Th

A Story about Life

And the tools that make it work

By Seth D. Hart

Dedication

It is only fair to dedicate this to a person that dedicated her life to

prayer and family. Katie Lee Hart, my Mom spent her life raising

children. She helped her Grand Mother raise her brothers and some

cousins during the Great Depression. Those were days that the

faith walk was a reality if one wanted to survive it was good to

have a viable prayer life. She married my Father James B. (Jimmy)

Hart right before World War II began. They had my older brother

James Bernard Hart JR and the journey for her and my Father

began. It was almost fifty years later when Dad passed on to his

reward. They had raised five children and they had grandchildren and great grandchildren. There was another son, Eddie five years after James and then I showed up January 1952. There were two sisters that arrived later, Katie and Mildred. There is a special connection between a Mom and her offspring. Dad may be a praying man but Mom seems to always know when something is going on with the kids. I believe that goes along with an incessant prayer life. My Mom turned ninety years old June 30 of 2013. I believe her prayers played a big role in us kids not having more problems and challenges than we had. For all the Moms and Grand Moms that may read this, don't give up on your kids and grandkids because your prayer isn't answered right away. Keep thanking God that his Word is true and then believe you will live long enough to shout the victory.

The Journey Begins

The Psalmist David talked about hiding the Word of God in his heart and I believe that is the key to being able to survive on a day to day basis. Ask anyone that has experienced the Alcoholics Anonymous journey and you will realize that sobriety happens on a day to day basis with help from a higher power as the alcoholic or addict understands it. When one makes a trip it is important to take tools along because there are bumps along the way that require fixing a flat or adjusting a belt. This requires tools. In life's journey a good tool to take is a copy of God's Word. Charles Spurgeon once said "If a person's Bible is falling apart their life probably isn't". Those are true words and they are viable to the process of having a safe and successful journey. . When I accepted Christ in April 1976 I asked him to place me where I could best serve him. I must admit he sent me some places that in the natural I would not have picked. I always ask for guidance and his perfect not his permissive will.

In Isaiah 55; 11 it says that Gods Word will not return void but will accomplish what it was sent to do. I believe wholeheartedly if you can count on anyone's word in the universe it is God's Word. Man at his best state is utter vanity and even the best of men will let a person down. In America products come with an owner's manual. The majorities of Americans tosses the manual in a drawer and never refer to it again unless they decide to file a lawsuit on the manufacturer. Read the manual for an electrical appliance and don't keep the radio to close to the bath tub. One would think that in itself is good judgment but for years people kept an electric radio close to a bath tub. I haven't heard a news report in years of anyone getting fried by a radio dropping into a bath tub. Have people quit taking baths? I would hope not nor have we as a nation gotten in such a hurry no one soaks in the tub anymore. I have always heard it was more sanitary to shower and wash the filth away as opposed to washing in it but each to his own I suppose. The upshot of the whole deal is read the owner's manual which for the believer is God's Holy Word, is it not? I saw a t shirt in Shreveport Louisiana that said when in doubt read the instruction book. That is some of the best advice I have seen or heard in years.

There is a lot of good common sense instruction in that book and the book even says that heaven and earth would pass away but Gods Word would not pass away. That is pretty solid and eternal so why do so many people resist reading its contents? Most American homes have a family Bible that sets on a coffee table or a plaque of Ten Commandments that hang on a wall. I guess that a nice gesture but how are we different than foreigners are that have cows walking around the streets that they won't kill and eat because in many cultures the cow is sacred so they can't partake of it. How many Americans do not open the book and feed and partake of its contents. We know that out of the Word of God flows life so why are some so hesitant to open and feed on its contents?

Why is prayer important because God has the hairs of our head numbered and he knows our needs before we ask so why bother asking? I often wonder how parents feel and many feel this way a lot when the children quit talking to Mom and Dad. I Thessalonians 5:16 -18 says; Always be joyful, never stop praying, be thankful in all circumstances, for this is Gods will for you who belong to Christ Jesus. If you have relatives that never call unless they are in trouble how do you feel?

Close friends recognize one another when they pick up the phone because there is relationship. Close friends are Gods way of apologizing for some of your kinfolks. Most families have an Uncle or some relative that they don't like to talk about. I believe sometimes God puts people like that in our life to challenge us to pray and believe our heavenly Father for a divine intervention. Families that have unsaved loved ones can pray that God put someone in their path that they will listen to and relate to. I believe our heavenly Father is merciful and he will send someone to everyone so on judgment day no one can say "I didn't have a chance".

II Chronicles 7; 14 says; If my people who are called by my name will humble themselves and pray and seek my face and turn from their wicked ways, I will hear from heaven and will forgive their sins and heal their land. I find it interesting that God is not talking to people outside the fold. He is talking to his people and I know with this being an old testament verse some would say he is addressing this to the nation of Israel and rightly so but the gentiles have been grafted in through adoption so wouldn't it apply to all Gods people? Prayer makes a difference and it even catches the attention of the secular community from time to time. The nation is in need of prayer and healing. It would be beneficial and a witness to the lost and unsaved community for just the Christians in the local community churches to meet for a day of prayer. Wouldn't it be refreshing to gather all the professing Christians in a community and just for one day put aside differences, cease from arguing and pray in one accord for the nation, state and local community? It could possibly cause a nationwide revival. Walk into any Dairy Queen in any town in any area of America and you will see a gathering of professing Christians. Sunday night fellowship and the gatherings sometimes are healthy unless there has just been a church business meeting. What kind of witness would it be to the community if there were several churches that were meeting and praying for the leaders just in the local community? It may very well change the whole atmosphere of the town.

Psalms 5; 2 says Listen to my cry for help, my King and my God, for I pray to no one but you. The Psalmist David by his prayer indicated he had no other gods before him. David was not perfect and it doesn't take a seminary education to understand that David missed it a few times. David knew his source and he prayed. I can remember a few years ago on super bowl Sunday I heard the announcer proclaim that this is the high holy holiday of the football religion. The teams come together and the fans take sides and the games begin. It is interesting to see how for a time that many people can put aside personal differences and come together to cheer their team on. I don't think God minds the believer to have a hobby or two if the hobby doesn't have them. Football in itself is not evil unless it takes the place of God in our lives. I don't think God minds the believer enjoying the game or other games as long as they don't take a person into sin. What if that many believers came together in one mind like the fans of a super bowl team than revival would sweep America.

Psalm 32; 6 says Therefore let all the godly pray to you while there is still time, that they may not drown in the floodwaters of judgment. Here is another verse where the godly are called to pray. God's people praying in one accord can accomplish great things. A few years ago I participated in an activity called the Walk to Emmaus. I witnessed a lot of good that came about as a result of individuals coming together for fellowship and study. I found out later that the success of these walks were due to around the clock prayer. The power of prayer is effective and I believe God honors the effectual fervent prayers of his children.

Mark 11; 24 says I tell you, you can pray for anything, and if you believe that, you will receive it, it will be yours. This was a scripture that was taught by Kenneth Hagin while he was living and was a launching pad for a Bible college in Oklahoma. I had never heard anyone that could teach on one Bible verse for an hour or better than could Kenneth Hagin. I believe there were many that thought he wrote that verse but of course he would tell anyone in a minute that was God's Word. Kenneth Hagin used that verse to bring him out of the bed of sickness when he was a boy. God honors his Word whether it's Kenneth Hagin speaking it or someone else. It is of utmost importance that the prayer be mixed with faith. When a person prays it is important to pray in faith believing.

Philippians 4; 6 says don't worry about anything; instead, pray about everything. Tell God what you need, and thank him for all he has done. It is important to be thankful and have an attitude of gratitude. God met his children's needs long before there was a Wall Street or a capitalistic or a socialistic government. Governments, organizations and anything built by man is temporary. If a person has lived any length of time at all they can remember names of companies that are no longer on the scene. Americans have enjoyed prosperity, benefits and retirement packages from many companies that no longer exist. These things are not bad as long as the believer has their priorities right. I believe God wants his children to be in health and prosper as their soul prospers. Priorities are the key and a relationship with our heavenly Father is foremost of importance.

There are many verses of scripture that admonish us to pray so it is obviously of utmost importance. The journey through life requires utilizing prayer as a constant companion. There is another tool that is important to take with you. Road maps are important and the Bible is an excellent map to take on ones journey through life. Would our creator send us on a journey and not provide a road map and a set of instructions?

If you don't know where you are going then you won't know when you get there. That seems like a no brainer but people stumble through life without a plan or a thought where the highway of life may take them. It is wisdom to chart a course and one way is to write ones goals down. There was a study of Harvard graduates over a fifty year period and the ones that wrote their goals down were the most successful. This was approximately 3% of the entire study. The reasons for success is that writing ones goals down is

Biblical Habakkuk 2;2 says Write the vision plainly on tablets so a runner can carry the message to others. Scholars that have studied the workings of the subconscious mind believe that when a person writes their goals or vision down it sends a message to the subconscious and it begins to work on a method to carry it out. Writing directions down and mapping out a plan is a good preparation for a successful journey.

Luke chapter 11 one of the disciples asked Jesus to teach them how to pray. This indicates that there is a right and wrong way to pray. If a person prays contrary to Gods will then how can God answer the prayer if by doing so it would violate his own word. Jesus instructs his disciples to forgive others as they ask for forgiveness. They are to ask for their daily bread. There are those in America that seem to take for granted there will always be bread on the shelves. Many Americans do not thank God daily for the many blessings we enjoy in America. One ice storm and the local stores can run out of bread rather quickly. Jesus goes on to instruct the disciples to perserver in their prayers. I believe praying specific and praying according to Gods will is important. One prayer in particular that would be out of Gods will is to ask God to save someone if it is his will. We know that it is not Gods will that any should perish so asking God to save someone if it is his will would be incorrect. Philippians 4; 19 says that he would provide all your needs according to his riches in glory by Christ Jesus. Notice he didn't say he would supply all ones greed. He instructs us against covetousness' so to pray to possess your neighbors spouse would be praying outside of Gods will when he has already admonished us not to be covetous. Study to show oneself approved and ask for wisdom and guidance in prayer is of utmost importance.

On the journey of life it is important to be discerning of messages one may receive. God uses imperfect people to do his perfect will but he will never send someone to teach something that is contrary to his word. There is a difference in having a spirit of discernment and a spirit of suspicion. When someone is expecting a settlement check they rarely inspect the deliveryman. The messenger may need a haircut and a shave as well as a new set of dentures. His uniform may be old and needing to be pressed as well as his shoes may need to be shined. The recipient is interested in that check and nothing more. The minister that is preaching the revival may have a good working knowledge of the word but there are people that will give that minister an inspection that rivals anything the military can conjure up. His hair may be thinning and his suit should have been professionally cleaned and pressed. God forbid John the Baptist shows up. Trash cans may be gold plated or galvanized but there is still trash inside. God looks at the inner and man looks at the outer. The speaker should be neat and clean for all purposes for the American pulpit but he may be a wolf on the inside. It would serve the parishioner well to have a good knowledge of the Word of God and evaluate a speaker as to his message lining up with the word, nothing more, and nothing less.

Why road maps are important; when someone sets out on a trip and they chart their course by a reliable road map their chances of getting to their destination successfully increases. There are occasions when a road map is revised and there may be changes and even changes in some highway numbers. It is important to check the map to be certain it is current by the date. The only thing that never changes is change. The Word of God is constant but other things may change. Highways get re-routed because of a change in traffic flow or maybe someone has figured a way to blast through a mountain and improve the highway. The traveler should stay up to date on changes in the highway system. In the course of life often times believers take an exit from the interstate of life. It may be an offense of sorts that take an individual down a side road. I can remember conversing with a man once that said he never missed a service until his youth director ran off with a lady from the church. He said when he did he took my religion with him. This is tragic and a story that is common sad to say. When people take their eyes off Christ and put them on people then they are set to take an exit off the interstate of life. This man was un-churched for over twenty years before he got back on God's interstate. He said he was glad God was gracious with him and helped him to get his eyes back on Christ and get his journey back on course. God's road map will help us stay the course if we check it from time to time as well as talk to the great cryptographer that put that map together. Stay on course by staying with God and his guidance.

Mothers are a great part of a person's journey through life; No measurement can be accurate enough to compare to a Mothers love. It runs deeper than anything known to the human race. It is undefinable and knows no bounds. Do not try to figure it out because you can't. Ever since the beginning when Eve was told she would bring forth children in pain Mothers have endured the pain. Years can come and go children grow up and leave home but some mothers still endure the pain. How do you think Mary felt as her son Jesus hung on the cross. Can you imagine her agony? How about you Christian or non-Christian? Have you brought your Mother agony or joy? Do you wait until Mother's day to call her and say thanks? Have you thought to do something nice for your Mom today, who knows if she will still be here Mother's day? There are some Moms that would appreciate flowers while they live.

Honor your Father and your Mother that your days will be long on the earth!

Why you picked the parents you did! I get a lot of eyebrows raised when I mention that because in the course of life I have heard individuals say "I didn't pick this"! You may not remember it but you did. Your parents are not perfect because if they were you wouldn't learn anything. I believe this earthly existence is a school and I believe that we have free will and we chose to come here. I will go one step further and say you picked your parents because it was part of your study plan for life 101. Americans do not always believe that but more and more of them are starting to realize that there is more going on than being born, reproducing and dying. There is a shift in consciousness and more people are becoming aware that earth is a preparation for something else. I believe Christ is our helper and the author and finisher of our faith but I also believe we have to do our part. I picked my Mom and Dad because their personalities are almost extreme opposites. My Dad could have written the book on tough love. I can remember him telling us boys that if we ever went to jail not to waste our one phone call on him. He said "I will laugh at you". You got yourself in so get yourself out. We were not given allowances when we were at home. If we wanted money for the show or something else we could pick up pop bottles or gather pecans or scrap iron. There were some good things that came with that. We had to look for legitimate legal ways to earn money and there were opportunities around. He fell a little short in the relationship area because I never saw him at any sport functions. I can never say we went hungry because we always had food and shelter. It got a little exciting around there somewhat but I can in no way demonize the guy because he done some good. My Mom had a heart of gold and would always help anyone that came along. That can be good and bad because there is a time when everyone needs a hand up but it doesn't need to be a permanent arrangement. I believe it was James Dobson that said it may be good for the young ones to rebel a little else they would have their feet under your table when they were forty. That is a good point because Mom and Dad won't always be there so the young ones need to learn to stand on their own. There can be balance between the two parents and many good lessons learned.

The journey of life can provide opportunities to pick up some habits both good and bad. Americans in their many travels around the country exit to refuel their vehicles and their bellies. The majority of Americans don't eat right and then there is that after meal smoke. When I was a boy I didn't know many people that didn't smoke. I lit up first time when I was thirteen years old. I can remember buying a pack of lucky strike non filters for eighteen cents at a little grocery store. That has been awhile back. It is now a little more expensive to shorten your life with something you buy. My Father died May 1990 and one year later I wrote an article for the paper about smoking. I would like to include it into this book about journeys in life.

Don't ever start!

Editor;

I feel like this letter may be interesting to your readers due to the effect tobacco and the use thereof affects people.

One of my Fathers favorite sayings when referring to people whom he felt had slighted him was, "That is a total lack of consideration and appreciation".

May twentieth 1990 my Father left this world for his eternal reward. He was seventy two and one half years old and many would say he lived a full life. Considering his tobacco habit it was a full life indeed. He was fortunate in the fact his death was sudden and he suffered little. I am thankful for that and I am sure he is also.

Some tobacco users are not so fortunate. Some people have slow agonizing deaths. My Father was one of the fortunate ones. The thing that is so upsetting is that after so many years of faithful support to the tobacco industry they didn't even send a thank you card.

Dad started smoking at around age fifteen. He was faithful in his support of the tobacco industry. He took his smokes everywhere he went. During World War II he left my Mom and my older brother and went off to serve in the south pacific theatre of operations in our war with Japan. His smokes went with him. That was one darling he wasn't going to leave behind.

No one ever accused him of not enjoying his tobacco habit. He inhaled everything he smoked, cigars, cigarettes, and even his pipe tobacco. He would inhale deeply, smile euphorically, and advise those around him "don't ever start".

He enjoyed his habit. Tobacco wouldn't sell if it were not enjoyable. He was one of the fortunate ones. He died quickly, many others do not. I have seen some people eaten up with cancer much younger than him. I had an Uncle that died in his fifties eaten up with cancer. I don't think there was a representative from any of the tobacco companies that dropped by to say thanks.

If the truth was known the high rollers that run the tobacco companies probably don't even use their own products. They know it is made to sell so let the buyers beware.

I don't have a beef with anyone who smokes. I used to smoke also until I decided I would rather enjoy my retirement money instead of the tobacco companies having it while I wasted away in some cancer ward. This is a free country, if you want to use tobacco, go ahead, buy them, smoke them, and enjoy them. But remember if you are one of the unfortunate ones who come down with a terminal illness don't hold your breath waiting for the tobacco companies to come around and offer to help you. Why should they? They have your money. It is your problem now.

My Dad supported the tobacco companies longer than he supported my mom or any of us kids. We attended his funeral but none of the people from the tobacco companies were there. I wouldn't be so naïve as to think they would really care. I think if you support someone for more than fifty years they should at least send a card.

But as my dearly departed Father would say! "That is a total lack of consideration and appreciation."

I accepted Christ and stopped abusing alcohol April 1976. It took me four more years to quit the tobacco habit. I used a Bible verse to help me kick the habit. It is Philippians 4; 13; I can do all things through Christ who gives me strength. God is no respecter of persons and if he helped me to quit he will help anyone. I believe if you open the door of your heart and ask him to come in he will.

There are a lot of traps on the journey of life, tobacco, alcohol, street drugs, and a smorgasbord of things that the enemy of our soul will use to snare the unsuspecting traveler. Make it a habit to ask God daily for wisdom and have your eyes open for the traps of the enemy. Remember if you get weary on the journey of life remember as the psalmist would say God will restore your soul when you trust him and you take a break from life and lie down in green pastures.

Isaiah 40:28-31 (NIV) 28 Do you not know? Have you not heard? The LORD is the everlasting God, the Creator of the ends of the earth. He will not grow tired or weary, and his understanding no one can fathom. 29 He gives strength to the weary and increases the power of the weak. 30 Even youths grow tired and weary, and young men stumble and fall; 31 but those who hope in the LORD will renew their strength. They will soar on wings like eagles; they will run and not grow weary, they will walk and not be faint.

This verse covers a multitude of areas for those who choose to have faith and why not. There is nothing wrong with going to a DR or a chiropractor or even a mental health professional. The exciting thing is that our heavenly Father never sleeps. He is available to converse with us any hour of the day or night. There is no appointment necessary and no secretary is going to tell you he has been called away. You don't have to worry about filing insurance or being concerned if your deductible has been met or if you are in the right group. He can have a conference with you 24/7 if you just have faith to reach out to him.

Stability in life; in this day of jets and super colliders one might ask the question. "Where is stability?" It should be sad to see that outside of God's Word and a faith in Christ there is no stability. Companies may come and go and stocks may ride and fall but the word of god is forever stable. Luke 21; 33 say "I tell you the truth... Heaven and earth will pass away but my word will never pass away. When we read this promise in the word of God we know that it is stable. We find stability in Christ our savior. We are comforted to know that God always takes care of his own children. Fret not yourselves of these unstable times; your heavenly Father has a word that will not pass away.

Vanity in Life, Ecclesiates 1; 2 says, "Vanity of Vanities, all is vanity." Throughout life everyone encounters someone who thinks they are a cut above everyone else due to social standing or numerous other reasons. Some people try to pretend they have wealth however, in reality they are like everyone else around them. It is amazing that some of the people who are worth the most amount of money are some of the friendliest down to earth people you could ever want to meet. The folks who try the hardest to impress someone are the ones who are usually in severe financial strains. What does this have to do with vanity? Well unfortunately some of Gods people fall into this trap of deceit. God wants his people to prosper but I don't believe he is pleased when his children snub some of his other children. A very wealthy old gentle man once said, "it doesn't cost anything to smile and speak". There are those who know how to take care of what God gives them and there are those that don't. Proverbs 16; 18 "Pride goes before a fall and a haughty spirit before destruction." The preacher was right. Vanities of vanities, all are vanity.

Storms in life; anyone whether it be a believer or a non-believer encounters some storms in life. Some folks will say they just don't seem to understand the meaning of these storms since they happen to everyone.. The Lord has some guidelines for the believer to follow. Matthew 5:44,45-46 says "Love your enemies, bless them that curse you, do good to them that hate you, and pray for them that despitefully use you and abuse you. That you may be the children of your father who is in heaven: for he makes the sun shine on the evil and the good, and sends rain on the just and the unjust. For if you love them which love you, what reward have ye? Do even the publicans the same? During the storms of life there is a temptation to do wrong. The believer has the knowledge to do right and should do right although it may be difficult at the time. Storms build character and we should thank God for the storms, they will make us strong in him as we learn to build our foundation on the solid rock.

Valleys in Life In the life of the believer there are valleys. In the life of an unbeliever there are pits. Without experiencing a valley it is hard to appreciate a mountain top. Our Lord experienced valleys and mountain tops so why shouldn't the believer experience the same. In the 23rd psalms David talked about a valley and the one who walked with him through the valley. I'd rather be a believer and experience a few valleys than to be an unbeliever and try to crawl out of the pits. If you will only believe then Christ will be with you through the valleys and you won't find yourself in the pits.

Should Christians enjoy sex? It is interesting some of the folks one can meet on the journey of life. I was taking to a man once about salvation and he said he had thought about getting saved and joining a church but if he and his wife did they could no longer enjoy sex because they were through having children. There was some well-meaning religious person had told him that unless you were trying to have children all sex for pleasure was sin. The Bible says in Proverbs the fifth chapter verse 18-19 let your wife be a fountain of blessing for you. Rejoice in the wife of your youth. She is a loving deer, a graceful doe. Let her breasts satisfy you always. May you always be captivated by her love? I looked that verse over and I couldn't find anything about her trying to get pregnant. This man thought the original sin was Adam lusting after Eve and the forbidden fruit was copulating with her. The scripture has a lot to say about it being OK for a man and his wife to enjoy sex within the boundaries of marriage. God wasn't being mean when he said to not covet your neighbor's wife. That was hazardous behavior long before a lot of the modern sexually transmitted diseases came along. Christians can give themselves permission to enjoy sex with their spouses.

Weapons on the journey; There are many weapons available today. Weapons have many purposes. Some are for game hunting and some are for use against people. One of the most powerful weapons known to the human race is the tongue. The tongue has probably caused as much destruction as all other weapons put together as well as the atomic bomb. James 3;6 says " The tongue is a fire, a world of iniquity; so is the tongue among our members, that it defiles the whole body, and sets on fire the course of nature; and it is set on fire of hell. The tongue like a kitchen match can be used for good or evil. Too many times people have been destroyed because of someone's loose tongue. Use your tongue as a weapon of spiritual warfare, destroying Satan and his demons rather than the precious children of God. Today's reflection: How am I using my tongue?

Intercessory prayer is important on our journey through life. The time it takes to sacrifice some time daily to intercede for someone is beneficial. This could save their life and probably has saved numerous lives if we only knew the impact it would amaze us.

1 Timothy 2:1 - I exhort therefore, that, first of all, supplications, prayers, intercessions, [and] giving of thanks, be made for all men; this verse makes me think about our elected officials. It is easy to pray for someone you like but if that person is a part of a political party we don't like well our prayer may not be as intense. It is important to pray for those in positions of authority whether it is national or local because what they do affects us. Let's pray that they make good decisions.

Romans 8:26 - Likewise the Spirit also helps our infirmities: for we know not what we should pray for as we ought: but the Spirit itself makes intercession for us with groaning's which cannot be uttered. More than one person has awakened during the night and had someone on their mind; it may be and many times is a family member and oftentimes a child. We can ask the Father to give us wisdom and see how we need to pray. Praying for their safety is a pretty good choice because most individuals need prayer in that area.

Ephesians Chapter 6

10 Finally, my brethren, be strong in the Lord, and in the power of his might. This comes about by consuming scripture.

11 Put on the whole armor of God that ye may be able to stand against the wiles of the devil. Wisdom is important in this arena because the devil has at least six thousand years of experience with lying. Ask God for discernment.

12 For we wrestle not against flesh and blood, but against principalities, against powers, against the rulers of the darkness of this world, against spiritual wickedness in high [places]. You

cannot punch the devil in the face with your fist but you can bruise him by using the Word of God on him.

13 Wherefore take unto you the whole armor of God, that ye may be able to withstand in the evil day, and having done all, to stand. Once the believer taps into the Word of god and gets the revelation knowledge needed for this project then speak the word and stand.

14 Stand therefore, having your loins girt about with truth, and having on the breastplate of righteousness; Speak the truth every man to his neighbor.

15 And your feet shod with the preparation of the gospel of peace; spreading the gospel is the job of every believer.

16 Above all, taking the shield of faith, wherewith ye shall be able to quench all the fiery darts of the wicked. Without faith it is impossible to please God. You can't stop a bird from landing on your head but you can decide if he builds a nest there.

17 And take the helmet of salvation, and the sword of the Spirit, which is the word of God: The sword of the spirit is important to take on ones journey.

Jude 1:20 - But ye, beloved, building up yourselves on your most holy faith, praying in the Holy Ghost; the believer can build themselves up and can do it by exercising their faith.

James 4:7 - Submit yourselves therefore to God. Resist the devil, and he will flee from you. If the believer is not submitted to God than trying to combat the devil in the spirit may not be successful.

Peter Chapter 2

13 Submit yourselves to every ordinance of man for the Lord's sake: whether it be to the king, as supreme; obeying the laws of the land is something the Christian should do.

14 Or unto governors, as unto them that are sent by him for the punishment of evildoers, and for the praise of them that do well. The Christian should not have to worry about the authorities if they are complying with the laws of the land.

15 For so is the will of God, that with well doing ye may put to silence the ignorance of foolish men: The Christian gives the naysayers less to talk about if they are trying to be correct.

16 As free and not using your liberty for a cloak of maliciousness, but as the servants of God. The Christian needs to keep in mind that they are servants and representatives of God.

Relationships

It is always interesting how a person can get the same information from two different people and come up with a different interpretation. Relationship has a lot to do with the entire scenario. A good relationship with ones parents is paramount to having a good relationship with our creator. It is important for a man to have a good relationship with his wife. First Peter 3 verse 7 says; Likewise ye husbands, dwell with them according to knowledge, giving honor unto the wife , as unto the weaker vessel, and as being heirs together of the grace of life; that your prayers be not hindered.

Recognition;

In life's journey there are encounters with different type individuals. There are folks that thrive on recognition and there are those that would rather just get paid and stay out of the spotlight. There are titles that appeal to some and a good paycheck is something that appeals to others. Matthew 23; 12 says; "And whosoever exalts himself will be abased; and he that shall humble themselves shall be exalted." There are some individuals that will do anything to steal the show. The scripture is clear what it says about those individuals. When the Lord exalts someone it is because they first humbled themselves. If you are the type that seeks to glory in yourself, just remember what the Bible says about that. It doesn't hurt to recognize someone for doing a good service. One should be hesitant about patting themselves on the back. I believe God gives us our skills so giving God the glory is better.

Flexibility of the journey;

High winds will break an oak tree sometimes. The tree can be rooted deep and may not be destroyed and weather the storm with a few broken limbs. Willow trees can be plucked up but a hard wind will bend the willow but it will usually spring back. The believer should be well rooted and grounded but be flexible enough to withstand the wind like a willow tree and bounce back. When should the believer be flexible? Flexibility is an asset during trials and tribulations. The believer should always be attuned to the spirit of God. When Joseph and Mary were looking for a room and Christ's birth was imminent they had to be flexible and take what accommodations were available. Joseph and Mary were certainly flexible and utilized a stable. Later on as Jesus started his earthly ministry he and the disciples utilized different type accommodations. Matthew 8; 20 says; "the foxes have holes and the birds of the air have nests but the Son of man hath not where to lay his head." Jesus was telling those around him if they were to follow him they were to be flexible. Many missionaries may experience facilities that are less than comfortable. How serious are you about serving Christ. Are you flexible?

How powerful the spoken word.

Most Americans are familiar with the creation story. We are made in God's image and we know God said let there be light and so forth. God spoke and it happened. People are made in God's image and the words we speak have power whether we want to admit it or not. Have you ever heard someone talk themselves into doing something they knew was wrong? There are ideas and then there is a drawing board with plans. Try building anything without talking to someone. Designers of automobiles get an idea and then they draw a design. They instruct their helpers to gather materials and construct something. In essence they spoke it into existence. God provides the raw material and then people put it together. Words are powerful and if you don't believe it why do coaches give their players pep talks at half time. They don't normally go into the locker room and tell the team they can't win. They encourage one another and many times they win the game sometimes with seconds to spare. Look around you and see what people have spoken into existence. Psalms 82 verse six and seven says; I have said ye are gods; and shall of you are children of the most high God. But ye shall die like men, and fall like one of the princes. Notice the little g. people have a lot more power than what they realize and life and death are in the power of the tongue so think about what you are saying. It is better to bless than to curse.

Life affords many opportunities for growth and learning experiences. Books are available and hands on experiences as one learns things outside the classroom. Ask any individual what they learned after banging their knee into something. There are learning opportunities everywhere.

Seedtime and Harvest;

Genesis 8; 22 says while the earth remains, seedtime and harvest, and cold and heat, and summer and winter, and day and night shall not cease.

There is a cycle to things and seed time and harvest is part of it. There is a legend about a man named Johnny Appleseed. He went about planting apple seeds and years later there are apples being harvested because of his work. Whether or not there was a man named Johnny Appleseed or not there are apples growing because someone planted a seed. When one considers the power of a seed one can consider words. Words are spoken and sooner or later there is a harvest.

The sower sows the Word

Mark 4 verses 3-8

Behold a sower went out to sow; and it came to pass as he sowed, some fell by the wayside, and the fowls of the air came and devoured them up. And some fell on stony ground, where it had not much earth; and immediately it sprang up, because it had no depth of earth. But when the sun came up, it was scorched, and because it had no root it withered away, and some fell among thorns, and the thorns grew up and choked it, and it yielded no fruit, and others fell on good ground, and did yield fruit that sprang up and increased; and brought forth, some thirty and some sixty and some an hundred. This passage is a good picture of individuals even in today's world of how certain ones process God's Word. People make choices on how they receive the Word and what they do with it once they get it.

This booklet has not been lengthy but that in no way should affect its ability to be effective. The Word of God has stood the test of time and will be here when we mortal humans have passed from the scene. Revelations 3;20 says that he stands at the door of our heart and knocks; if any man hears his voice, and open the door, I will come in to him, and will sup with him, and he with me.

He is knocking at the door of your heart, will you let him in. The one who knows you best loves you most. His name is Jesus, King of Kings and Lord of Lords.